Amari Peters

Amaripeters123@gmail.com

REAL SEASONS OF MY LIFE

By: Amari Peters

Copyright Page:

RealSeasonsOfMyLife © Copyright <<2024>> Amari Peters

All rights reserved. No part of this publication may be reproduced, distributed, or transmitted in any form or by any means, including photocopying, recording, or other electronic or mechanical methods, without the prior written permission of the publisher, except with brief quotations embodied in critical reviews and certain other noncommercial uses permitted by copyright law.

Although the author and publisher have made every effort to ensure that the information in this book was correct at press time, the author and publisher do not assume and hereby disclaim any liability to any party for any loss, damage, or disruption caused by errors or omissions, whether such errors or omissions result from negligence, accident, or any other cause.

Adherence to all applicable laws and regulations, including international, federal, state and local governing professional licensing, business practices, advertising, and all other aspects of doing business in the US, Canada or any other jurisdiction is the sole responsibility of the reader and consumer.

Neither the author nor the publisher assumes any responsibility or liability whatsoever on behalf of the consumer or reader of this material. Any perceived slight of any individual or organization is purely unintentional.

The resources in this book are provided for informational purposes only and should not be used to replace the specialized training and professional judgment of a health care or mental health care professional.

Neither the author nor the publisher can be held responsible for the use of the information provided within this book. Please always consult a trained professional before making any decision regarding the treatment of yourself or others.

For more information, email Amaripeters123@gmail.com.

ISBN: (print only)

Dedication

To God who is the author and finisher of our faith. To my Mother, Chenequa, brothers, Xavier and Elijah, and sister, Anyah, for always believing in me and inspiring me to write this book.

Table of Contents:

Introduction………….. ……………..Page 5

Growing up……………. ……………Page 9

Trials and Tribulations……………. Page 25

Warrior Battles………………. …….Page 32

But God…………………………… Page 51

The New Me……….. …………… Page 75

Remember Who You Are……….. Page 89

All Glory to God…………………. .. Page 110

Acknowledgments………….. ….. .Page 117

Author's Bio……………… ………..Page 118

Introduction

My mom would always tell me, "Amari, find a problem and come up with a solution." I would see my classmates sitting alone. I could see that they desperately needed the love of the father. I wanted to share my faith. When I see others down and hard on themselves, I want to be the light on campus. Being filled with the compassion of the Lord, I wanted to see them happy and thriving. I wanted them to know who God says they are. I would encourage them. I would let them know God loves them ,that they matter ,and are important. I hope they all and you know God has a plan for you. It took a while for me to find the courage to open up and share the wonderful news with my classmates. I may have grown up in an environment that was unhealthy, But I'm grateful for it because it strengthened me. You may not control how others act, but you can make a difference and positively impact the lives of those around you. I feel like someone needed to hear that. Being the hands and feet of Jesus wherever God has you. Then something changed in me. I had never felt it before. All I had wanted to do was spend time in his presence and his name is Jesus Christ. Messiah. He is worthy of all my praise and the name above all names. So that I could be spiritually mature and know the bible. I taught what I know. God told me, "All you have is all you need." This is my story about a mellow girl who was fearless and full of courage. Ready to go on adventures with God. As I share how I went from broke, busted, and disgusted to living the blessed life God called me to live. I will give you practical tips on how you can grow and mature intol the best version of who God is calling you to be. So you can live out your walk with the Lord. No matter what age you are, God can still use you. It's not too late for you. Grab a snack. Find a comfortable spot in the house or recliner. Sit back and enjoy the journey of a shy girl who became the God-Fearing mature woman that God called her to be.

Letting Go Freely
by Amari Peters

I had to let go

Even though

It was hard

Was I going

To allow

My feelings

To take control

Or my faith

Because God

Was saying

Yes Daughter

It's time

For you

Peters/Real Seasons of My Life
To be free

To see

The truth

That you are

Valuable

_____

CHAPTER ONE:
Growing up

On October 6, 2000, I was born along with my twin sister, Anyah. We were born prematurely or, as my mama would say, "Her Miracle Babies" Our mom prayed for us day and night. Through her tears and frustration, God heard my momma's cries, and he brought us here. I thank God for my praying momma, who loved us so much. She sacrificed so much for us so we could be here. I thank God for keeping her and us. My mom always saw the best in us. She knew we would be something special. Do extraordinary things on this earth. That God put us here for a reason. It's an interesting story about how we got our name. Our nana (Our Mom's mom) was a registered nurse and amazing at watching us on the weekends. Both looked through an enormous book of baby names. They even found Amari and Anyah, which later on I later found out were biblical names. They would always tell me that no one had at the time! They rarely heard anyone named Amari and Anyah. Anyah means grace and favor. Amari means eternally lovely. The Lord knew we needed his grace always. Our story was a blessing from God. He also knew I needed that as a reminder of who was in him. My sister loved to sing. My mom would always say she would always sing anywhere and everywhere. She was very outgoing and loved to talk to everyone. I was always the shy one, and rarely talked to anyone. I was always with her. Anyah always inspired and encouraged me to be more courageous. Including to get out of my shell more by dancing. She just had that warm effect on people, always leaving them feeling happy and bubbly. If we had to stay with someone, I would cry, begging my mom not to leave. Giving her the puppy dog eyes. I loved and still love my mom. She is still like a best friend to this day. I will always respect her as my mom. So this was how me and my twin were born. We were always together, whether that was talking to each other. It would be from sunrise to evening. We were singing together in our room, listening to Radio Disney in our pre-teen years. We would listen to One Direction or Cody Simpson. There was never a dull moment, but there were a few struggles. Our relationship wasn't perfect. We would argue here and there over silly things, but always found our way back to laughing and sharing stories. We could share stories that would last a lifetime. We needed each other. I thank God for giving me a twin because when times get tough, I would talk to God and my bubbly twin. I knew she got my back, and I got hers. I would not let the hard times get me down. I didn't realize it then, but now I know God was working out everything for my good. I needed my twin for all that we would go through, all the trials and tribulations we went through at a young age strengthened us in the lord. Grew us closer to God. The Lord knew we needed each other. We were unstoppable together. To go through this amazing, indescribable, worth telling for generations to generations, this amazing story.

Anyah, she has helped me get through these hard seasons. I didn't see her disability with epilepsy, born with a limitation. I knew she could do more. Our mom taught her how to take care of herself from a young age. Everyone knows her as the "drama queen" she could put on a show. She would exaggerate every minor thing. But I loved how she was also bold. She would speak her mind, no matter who was watching. She was unfiltered. She inspired me to be authentic and my mom who told me what's the point if you don't be real in life or at counseling. Don't you want to be free? Healed. Also how Anyah felt. This is not to shame him. I am keeping in one hundred, real and true. Most of this took a lot of healing in my walk with the Lord to share this. But It's worth telling so others can know that there is hope, a light at the end of the tunnel and things are going to get better, little by little, day by day. You don't want to miss this!

Dad's House

Growing up, my family was dysfunctional, and it's funny how sometimes you could adjust to something so long that you're so comfortable you don't want to get out of it. Because you think it's normal, but it's not okay. My mom went through a lot with our biological father. When we weren't born yet, my mom separated from him because their relationship was getting very toxic and I won't go into detail here. Anyway, I rarely ever saw my dad. He did substances and things that were not good, but not around us. My dad would get the help needed, but would go back out occasionally to still do that. We would stay with him sometimes, our stepsisters and stepbrothers who were not beneficial influences on me, my sisters and my brother. We all would watch scary movies, explicit movies and tv shows that let's just say not of God. I repented because I did not want to give a doorway to the enemy or those spirits. I remember the first time we met our step brothers and step sisters, me and my sister just looked around at their house.

It was nice, but we felt like strangers. We rarely knew them and kind of didn't want to because we were so used to being with our mom twenty-four seven. We would go to church with him and it was nice. I enjoyed seeing the youth ministry singing and worshiping God. But it was hard hearing from my family that my dad was on drugs and couldn't spend time with him. We also stopped seeing our step-brothers and sisters because of the shows and movies they were watching. That's when I started praying for them and my dad. I saw God as my father. He filled those places of abandonment with his love and acceptance. But this took time. I was grateful for the time he spent with us. He would take us out to ear every blue moon. But I had to learn that he was doing the best he could to love us. I thank God for keeping my dad so he could get right with him. So he could take him seriously. I would love it when he would tell me I love you, young women of God. It made me feel comforted, safe and loved, like I was somebody.

"6742" As we like to call it

My stepdad came into my life years later when I was about eleven years old. After my mom separated from my biological dad. Also, in case you are wondering, they never got married. Back to the story. Mr. J (Our stepdad) was kind of nice at first, buying us chocolate milk, taking us out to eat, then he became very strict once they got married. He was rarely home, always out doing his gigs as a DJ. Our mom would stay home and watch us. He was very strict with us. He was a little harsh with how he said things. Also, I did not care if he liked me or not because I knew that my worth comes from Christ. He really didn't like my brother. I don't know why, but that made my brother feel rejected. Mr. J was more meaner and stricter on him. But we had some good moments. He would make us laugh, fix us some amazing African food and we would listen to popular songs such as Hannah Montana's "Party in the USA" on repeat. This made us appreciate him once we saw that, to some extent, he loved us. We may not like him because of the pain he caused, but we still love him. Through this, I learned to forgive my dad and my stepdad. It was not, but in this next chapter, I will explain how I learned to forgive him and my biological father and give him to the Lord.

"Forgiveness"

I forgive my dad and stepdad. I let that anger and rejection go. I gave it to God. So I can be free and healed. I said, lord I will give them to you. I trust you got them. I pray we reconcile. I had to declare that I was healed from rejection and hurt. So I didn't have to carry that weight of bitterness and resentment because the more you hold on to unforgiveness, the more it ages you. Someone wise told me that. Similarly, let me take you back to a time before I even moved in "6742" This was when my mom was a single mother, living with her best friend and their kids, When I was in elementary school. This was a lot because we had to move in with complete strangers who weren't excellent influences. I would question God. I am trying to do right. Where are the Godly friendships? But little did I know God was sharpening me, strengthening me and teaching me how to become that iron sharpens iron friend. So when me and my cousins would watch things and listen to music. We would always get in trouble for something we didn't do, but because we were with them, we all took the blame for it. But I don't judge because no one's perfect even if I'm not, sadly. But I know they were hurting, getting out of foster care from an early age and moving in with their guardian. You know, hurt people hurt people. So how can I even be mad? They were doing what they knew, that was their coping skill, which made them feel accepted by getting in trouble. It was their way of living. Surviving. I pray God heals them. I wanted to let you know if you are going through this, things will get better, keep your head held high. You change, encourage your friends to do the right things, make excellent choices because they will save you a ton, later on in the actual world. You will make it. It wasn't an accident that you're reading this book. God ordained it. I hope you feel inspired, hopeful. Better days are coming, better days are here.

You are safe. You are in the abundance and overflow of God.

"Lust and Redemption"

My friend was always learning, always buried in his books, his glasses perched on his nose. He was constantly bettering himself, and I admired that about him. He inspired me to grow in every area of my life. He knew almost everyone in the neighborhood, always the social one, always with something to say. One night, we were playing hide-and-seek in the closet, and we kissed. It was innocent at first, but soon feelings began to develop between us. But before you jump to conclusions, let me clarify: we never went any further. We didn't act on those feelings, if you know what I mean. Still, something didn't sit right with me about the whole thing. At the time, I didn't understand that lust had begun to take root in my heart. I didn't want to kiss him. I didn't want those feelings. But that lust—it was still there, attached to me like an invisible weight

I couldn't shake. I didn't learn how to control it until I was much older, in my late teens. It feels good to finally get this off my chest and share it with someone who may be going through something similar. I'm so grateful to God for protecting me because things could have easily spiraled out of control. Things could have gone in a much darker direction. But God watched over me, keeping me from straying too far down that path. My family raised me in the Lord. We went to Vacation Bible School, and my mom even led a women's group. We prayed to God every day, and wrote to Him in our journals. But sin doesn't care about your background. It doesn't discriminate. It sneaks in when you least expect it. And lust? Lust came so subtly. It just appeared, and I didn't even realize what was happening. Soon, I started watching things online—things that were just a click away. I was bored, seeking something to fill the emptiness. I wanted to be accepted, but my stepdad was rarely around, and my siblings and I didn't know how else to reach out to our parents. At times all I had was God. I want to encourage every parent reading this: check on your kids. Make sure they're doing okay. I didn't tell my mom because she didn't want to hear it. It made her feel like I let her down. As if I wasn't her perfect child. I'll admit, it's hard for me to share this part. It's so personal, but I know someone needs to hear it. I would bottle up my emotions, keeping everything inside. But when I couldn't hold it in anymore, I'd go to God. In my quiet time, I would surrender it all to Him. He is the Prince of Peace, and He is the only one who can heal the broken parts of us. It's in him that we are free. Free from lust. Allowing God to clean you from the inside out. He can then help you to become the new creation that he called you to be. Then you go from healed to delivered by the power of God. You can overcome any addiction from drinking to cussing. Can anyone relate to this? I know it's not easy to admit, but if my story helps just one person, then it's worth sharing. You are not alone. I tried so many times to stop watching those things, to turn away from it, but it was hard. Once you're entangled in something for so long, it feels almost impossible to break free. But God. It took the Great I Am, the King of Kings and Lord of Lords, to deliver me. He gave me the strength I didn't have on my own. Through years of counseling, mentorship, and leaning on God's Word, I finally began to break free. The Bible says, *"I can do all things through Christ who strengthens me."* And with Christ, I realized I could overcome lust. God can deliver you, too. I cried out to God, asking Him to heal me. *"By His stripes, I am healed."* I would pray, *"God, take this lust from me. Remove the cravings, remove the desires that lead me down the wrong path."* I want to encourage you to find someone you trust—whether a close friend, a mentor, or a counselor—someone you can talk to face-to-face. It makes a difference. You may not want to share your struggles, but the Bible says, *"You shall know the truth, and the truth will set you free."* How can you be set free if you don't first understand the root of your struggle? Pray, *"Lord, help me develop a deeper love for You. Father I know the root cause is rejection because I did not have my dad in my life. So God I ask you to fill me with your love. Fill those places that my dad left wounds with your peace. That you calm my soul and my mind. That only you can heal my soul from the hurt and pain from my dad in my life. Purify me from the inside out. Change my heart, my desires, so that everything I do brings glory to You."* For God was with me through it all. For he was working all things out for my good, even when I couldn't see it. He was there, protecting me every step of the way. Slowly one by one God started healing me.

Mom's Words
by Amari Peters

I remember

Mom's Words

That lifted

Me up

In one of the

Most hard times

Mom's Words

Inspired me

Even when

I felt rejected

By Society

Mom's Words

Kept me going

Peters/Real Seasons of My Life
Helped me to Believe

In the lord

Mom's Words

Reminded me

That God loves me

_____

CHAPTER TWO:

Trials and Tribulations

I would highly advise kids to read with adult supervision as I'm about to talk about some vulnerable topics. One day me, my siblings and cousins. We all were having quality time with each other, playing games, eating nutritious food and meeting new people. It was nice just to be a kid. Then I went into the room, me being innocent and naive thought he was just going to say hi, then we would go back and enjoy the party. It was only him and me in the room. Somehow, things went south real quick. He started touching me in places that I shouldn't have been. All I remember is that I was wearing brown tights. I wanted to leave, to get out, but didn't know how to stand up for myself. I was shy. At that moment, I wanted to escape, to run. But I didn't and remembered I left and went out of the room. Feeling shame, guilt, and condemnation come in. I kept it the whole night and didn't tell anyone. How could I? I didn't want to make my mom feel sad because she was already going through? But later on I found out it hurt her for me not even telling her because then she would let me go to counseling and get the help I needed to become whole and healed. I didn't know how to tell her at first, but the more I opened up to her little by little. I was more comfortable around her and felt so much relief after I told her. Then God healed me and my mom's relationship. I had learned over time she was fighting her own battles, then realized she wasn't spending as much time with me and my siblings, so after some time I saw her being aware of how we were doing and checking up on us often. Also, I want to mention just as I was bold and spoke up for what was right; I encourage you to speak out and speak up. Don't make the enemy let you feel shame, guilt, or less than because God wants you to live in peace and in freedom. Talk to someone, don't be afraid to share. Remember, you can always talk to Jesus and surrender it to him and allow him to heal you through his word.

"Second Grade"

I was lying down one night reminiscing over the words in my head, "You got held back" This adversity shook me, but I overcame it. Even though I got held back in second grade, I didn't let that stop me from pursuing my dreams. My teacher thought I wasn't ready to go on to the next level only because she felt I wouldn't be able to pass the standardized tests. Imagine telling that to a nine-year-old, that hurt. I remember going home that night crying, sobbing, and wondering, "Why does everybody else get to go on except me? Was there something wrong with me? Why am I always last? I was only in the second grade. As time went on, I started feeling unimportant, like no one even cared because my grades were average, and I did not care, because I had to repeat the second grade. So why even try? Who would understand me? Was there even hope? Until one memorable afternoon, my Mother sat down with me and said," Amari, don't let that stop you. God has greater plans in store for you. God will use this for his glory. Your purpose was divinely ordained, and God is orchestrating events for your benefit. Your story is not over." That's when I knew it was time to buckle down and get serious, to improve my grades. Entering my eighth-grade year, I started learning more about my faith and who I am in God. That I was loved by God and how he cares for me. With him I can be successful. For nothing is to hard for God. I was studying late nights to make sure that I am doing the best that I can do. Unto the lord. Asking God for his help every step of the way. At the end of my eighth-grade year, when I went to discover my grades, I found out I got all A's. I was so excited and proud of myself. From that moment on, I knew that I could do anything I put my mind to, if I only believed. Writing this book, I want to encourage others around the world and let them know that they are important. Also, tell others about my faith, giving them a light in their darkness. That I know what it feels like to feel alone, hidden and kind of like the underdog. You feel always left out and how God, My heavenly father, my Mom, My best friend and My siblings who helped me to see everyone deserves a second chance. My mentors saw the best in me and helped me to walk with confidence and live the God-ordained life he called me to live. He helped me to overcome those hard obstacles. I had to surrender and be vulnerable to him. It was in my authenticity and vulnerability that I found true peace and freedom. Even though I got held back in second grade, I didn't let that stop me. I kept growing, learning, maturing, into the beautiful youthful women of faith, telling everyone about Jesus Christ, my Lord and savior.

Content

by Amari Peters

Seeking for approval

Validation

From my Education

People

Places or things

That don't even bring

Me comfort

But

When the light

I so desperately

Long for

Sings to the broken heart

That is now healing

As she allows Christ her

Peters/Real Seasons of My Life
Savior to purify her heart

Mind-body and soul

Peeling back the hurt and pain

CHAPTER THREE:

Warrior Battles

I wanted to encourage you and let you know that you are not defined by man, things, or what others have labeled you as in your past. You are defined by who God says you are. You are justified by faith. You are a Daughter/Son of the Most High King, Jesus Christ the Messiah. If you let him, he can change you for the better, help you do better, and transform you into the person he's called you to be. I remember, through all my hurt and pain. God still had a plan. I needed God to help me, to purify me of all my sin, shame, guilt, and condemnation. Can anyone testify? I remember the early morning of my sixth-grade summer early morning. Me and my sister were getting ready for the day of camp, eating a healthy breakfast. This the most important part of your day. When the world was sleep, I was up doing my Devotion. I was reading my bible and talking to God. While God was talking back to me. Encouraging me and telling me how much he adores me. That he is with me every step of the way. Then as we got on the bus to our church, we were in for a treat. I sat with my cousin, my twin and our youth pastor on the other side. We were all having a good time. As we stepped foot on the rocky sand, we felt the heartwarming sun as it shined on our glowing faces. Our camping staff gave us a warm welcome. We were safe. We felt like we belonged. Like we could pour out all our secrets and not feel ashamed or judged. Ready to let go, have fun, and experience the love of the Father, Jesus Christ. They were playing our favorite Christian music. Our camp counselor was kind and sincere. It felt nice to know that there were more like-minded people than me. I remember there I felt so loved, accepted, and safe. The first night in our cozy vintage cabin beds was amazing. We all sang songs, wrote in our journals, talked to God, and had our devotional time in a group. We worshiped the Lord together and got out of our comfort zones; I went canoeing for the first time. The station supervisor and my camp friends thought we were pros at it. It was a Long-lasting and Life-changing experience. Here I was free. Free to be free from my chains of shame and insecurity. I remember one night, in particular, we were doing our devotional time, and then after one by one, she talked to us. I shared with her the battles I faced and all the hardships I wanted to run all away from. But she reminded me that there was a man who bled and died with nails in his hand for me. So I can be free and accepted, knowing in his eyes I am not less than. I am not a mistake. But perfect. God has the very best in store for me. He has the very best intentions for me. That he is there for me twenty-four seven and he will never leave me. I couldn't believe it was this angel from heaven. It's like she knew everything I had been through and answered in a way that made me feel secure with God and know that God is with me and he will forgive me. That all my sins were completely erased. I could start a brand new day. Chapel gosh! Guys, the chapel was amazing. We could feel the love of God, God was in the room. It was so peaceful. Amazing youth pastors spoke that night, lives were touched and transformed for the better. I dedicated and surrendered my life to God, asking him to come into my heart and help me live right and cleanse me from the inside out. God had began to become real to me. That morning, sadly, I had to go back home and face the challenges up ahead, but this time I was coming back strong and fearless. The seed of faith was planted; it just needed to be watered and blossom into beauty. As we said our goodbyes and went home, something happened. I couldn't explain it. It was so peaceful, so compassionate, all I could be a sad cry. Like I would miss that experience cry. Like God, don't leave me. But little did I know that he was with me, he was for me and he was comforting me at that moment. Even when I was in the store, I couldn't stop crying. Some of it had to do with feeling accepted, feeling accepted by the love of God, gosh! It was, so pure and genuine, also accepted by others who had a heart for God, it was So amazing. I will never forget that moment. That week of church I gave my life to Jesus Christ and accepted him as my Lord and savior. It was a blessing to know that I had someone to do life with because even though I used to feel lonely I wasn't alone. When

Jesus stepped on the scene everything changed. Little by little God started filling me with his truth, and most of all the word of God, helping me to grow and mature from that old, insecure person to a new pure and redeemed and whole Godly woman. I said "Lord use me. I am a willing vessel" Now I want to encourage you if you ever feel alone you have a friend in Jesus who loves you so much. He sees you and will never leave you and he has great plans in store for you. So you can be free from your insecurities, worries, fears, anger, hurt and condemnation. He is loving, kind and genuine. He corrects in love and will never stop loving you unconditionally.

"Entering Middle School"

When I walked through the doors of the hallway. I could feel my adrenaline running, my heart filled with joy and happiness. Leaving all my "Childish ways behind" I was ready to embark on the recent journey of life called middle school. For me, middle school wasn't all bad. I met some amazing people, teachers and made long-lasting friendships. Hopper was a nice and big school. I remember it taking me a while to find my classes on the first day of school. Then I saw quite a few familiar faces from my elementary school, So I knew where my next classes were. I remember Emily loved to sing. She was so kind and sweet. Alexandria, who loved to smile and make everyone laugh. I remember Kristina ,who loved to draw. I mean, this girl should win America's most talented artists, painters or something. Celeste who loved to draw with her skater outfit and beanie outfit on. (I loved her style, It was so cool!) I will never forget Erika. Me and her were in choir together. I loved choir so much, especially the pop show, getting to sing popular songs at the moment such as, "Dynamite" by China Anne McClain and One Direction, "That's what makes you beautiful". Wonderful memories. I had a pretty cool teacher such as Ms Woest who was a down-to-earth science teacher, also my after school mentor, who was so nice. Now

Mr. Toliver was my the teacher, who was strict, he didn't play, I remember one time, we were getting a little loud in the class, then He banged his clipboard. It got our attention. It scared me. but I sure did pay attention. I remember Mr. Langston, you all! Almost every girl in the class had a crush on him because he had these handsome blue eyes. He taught history. He was so nice and kind to everyone in the class. We all sure paid attention. I remember Ms. Ramirez was nice too. She taught English class. My friends used to call me a teacher's pet because I would always stay focused on my schoolwork and pass my classes. But I did not let that get to me. In this class I would finish an essay so fast. If it was a topic I loved, I would plan my outline. This saved a ton of time. That's what I used to write in this book too. It really helps you to narrow down your book and keep you focused on the message you're trying to convey. Anyway, Ms. Ramirez would give me the class dojo. It was to conduct our score. Some of my friends got jealous because I was finishing first and could have free time mid- beginning of the class. They started talking behind my back about me. This led to a friendship that ended and I distanced myself from them and enjoyed spending time with my mom. I helped her with her photography business. I realized that I am worth too much to waste my time with friends who weren't even for me. I prayed for them and kept my eyes on the lord. Also, did I mention at this point in my life, I was spending time with Jesus but didn't at the time. I wasn't making him a priority like I should. I didn't really know the importance of valuing my relationship with Jesus Christ and keeping him first. I valued him, but I'm glad I showed his qualities such as encouraging and uplifting others in christ. Then something unexpected happened: my life was moving so fast. We packed out of the driveway, with our clothes and all in the driveway and pulled into Golden Corral, not knowing where to go next. We were homeless. With only three hundred dollars. My mom, worried, wondered what she was going to do, what were we going to do. Then she prayed and trusted God, that everything was going to be alright. Then she called all the homeless shelters and they were all filled. Then we found one that was affordable. One that God had for us, you could say heaven sent, the provision stage. One that I will never forget.

"Wanting Acceptance"

When I tell you guys God provided for us. I thank God for always keeping us and watching over us. God is with us daily. He is a wonderful dad. My best friend is him. He is my number one supporter. Lord, let not my will be done, but yours. I pray the lord guides you and leads you on the right path. To share God's goodness: I want to share the amazing goodness of God without bragging. I want you guys to know that God will provide for your situation, if it may not happen on your timing, but his timing is perfect. It says in Philippians 4:19, "God will supply all your needs according to his riches in glory" No matter what you're going through, God will get you through. He is your strength. Cling to him and he will guide you and lead you on this blessed journey called life. I remember God sending people who rarely knew food, canned goods, etc. The church gave us money and food. I started going to seventh grade. The school I went to was campbell middle school. Our school gave us resources on food pantries and it was a miracle because the people were so nice and kind. We stayed in that hotel for some time and stayed with our mom's friend from time to time. It was a lot because they had their own family, but we all made it work. I'm so grateful and appreciative for them. We also had to go back to school. The beginning of seventh grade was hard because we moved schools and I barely knew anybody. I made some cool friends who inspired me to be in a book club and love to read. We would always recommend books to each other. We would meet up before school and go to the library. During lunchtime we would talk to our librarian who was the coolest. She was so down to earth and gave us the tea on upcoming recent books she recommended. We also went on book field trips, where we got to meet the authors of the book. I will never forget it. It inspired me to also want to write a book one day and inspire the millenials to take care of their mental health. Also, I remember Mr. Mondesir. He was so caring, so nice and compassionate. He made history fun, he made us want to learn history. I saw him as a father figure because, number one, he had a relationship with the lord. He was really down to earth and loved me as his daughter in Christ. He was there for me. I thank God for him because at that time I was overcoming depression and anxiety. I feel less than and unworthy, shame. He taught me to love others with Christ's love and to forgive those who may have hurt you. So I can be free, learning to love myself as God loves me. Blessed and restored. My faith grew in the lord because I and my family started spending time together. We started having family prayers together in the morning. We would put on praise and worship songs and praise God. We thanked him for all he has done in our lives. He's been so good. He kept us and watched over us. He made sure I was always taken care of. That I had everything I needed. For he truly was lord in my life. That season of homelessness really sharped on faith in God. We learned that through the good or bad God is still God. We learned to seek God with all our hearts. Not just by what we say but our actions. It took time, but God is patient and a rewarder of those who diligently seek him. So when you seek God, seek him with everything that is within you. With all your heart, mind, will and emotions. Then watch God move like only he can move. Doing miracles, signs and wonders because you love him and have a heart for him. He is faithful and will answer your prayers.

"The signs"

Eighth grade was the time where I was supposed to be having fun, enjoying my last year and making memories. But the second semester was very difficult at times. Even though it was my last year, I was still wanting that acceptance. So desperately I wanted to fit in. To feel loved. God was still watering that seed from my youth camp counselor. I would get in the word of God and allow God to speak life into me. Then my sad and gloomy days turned into joyous and cheerful days. I am learning it's all about perspective. I remember this guy, named James. We became friends. We would sit by each other almost every day at lunch. He was very kind and nice and knew the lord. But, something was still missing. He loved God. He would say things that weren't good and weren't really on the same level as I was in the lord. Me, being young and desperate for attention still wanted to be friends, I still would be around him. We would meet up after school, walk and talk at the bus stop. Never Kiss Thank God! We were young and didn't know the essence behind courting. Doing things God's way. I was still growing little by little in the lord. I began to become obsessed with him to the point where I would meet him after school and run after him to the bus. Ladies, can we be real? Let me give you some tips if a guy doesn't want to pursue you and you keep trying to pursue him. Let him go Hunnie! It is time for you to move on. Develop a relationship with the lord becoming one with God. Work on growing with God. Allowing God to fill you with his wisdom, self discipline, and strength. I had found in christ. Worship and reading the word was my greatest weapon. Also, once you put God second place, Where he is meant to be first place in every area of your life. It's like saying the man is the one who saved you or is your savior, which is a dangerous thing. Man is not perfect. They make mistakes. God is perfect, Saves and can heal you to the point where you are thriving in your purpose. So that when God brings the right man along you won't run him off. But set boundaries and keep the lord at the center of your relationship and let the word of God become your standard. Anyways, Let me tell yall about Ms. Duffus! Senorita Duffus was so nice, sincere and kind. She was so sincere and caring. She taught Spanish and did an excellent job. She loved all of us as her own students. I will never forget her praise and shout dance. She would do it before her students would take their test, So she could get some time to herself. She was very structured. I liked that about her. She loved what she taught and it was evident in her lessons. She always made it fun and interesting. Whether that was through an encouraging video or funny alphabet song we had to learn. Ms. Duffus made me want to do better, to be better and to improve. She really admired my love for the Lord because I was a light on campus. I got to class on time. I gave all glory to God for that because if it wasn't for the lord raising me with an amazing God-fearing mother and God Surrounding me with teachers who love the Lord, I don't know where I'd be. Mr. Eisenberg was my math teacher who was the cool teacher that everyone wanted. He was very caring of his students and had a heart to serve. He encouraged me when I felt as if I was behind in his class. Letting me know that I am not less than or a failure just because it may take me more time to understand the material than other students. I thank God for him. I could name countless other teachers but I wanted to encourage yall and let yall know the best is yet to come.

You can do anything you put your mind to. You are more than a conqueror. You are not a mistake. You are perfect in God's eyes. Keep your head held high. Don't ever let anyone tell you that you are nothing or worthless because those are lies from the enemy. The word of God says you are a child of God, You are adopted into Christ kingdom. You are a new creation in Christ, the old ways, habits you are gone. You are victorious. In this next chapter I will go on to explain about highschool and the creeping depression that tried to find its way back in. I will give tips on how to overcome it.

Hidden
by Amari Peters

Always put in the back

Seen as an outcast

Peters/Real Seasons of My Life
Never taken seriously

Who would like to know me

For me

Judged by first appearance

Wouldn't give me a chance

I want to be their friend

How can I let them know

Who gets me

I am always called on last

Last in line

Last in races

Last in life

Who will chose me

Who notices me

Who accepts me

Who hears me

My cries

tears day and night

Peters/Real Seasons of My Life
Someone please

Accept me for me

And not judge

based on how I look

By the clothes wear

Or my beautiful afro hair

But at the end of the day

He comes to my rescue

Time and time again

To say I love you

And you are mine, I am yours

I belong to Christ

My lord and savior

As I listen to his voice

I know I'm going to be alright

Just holding his hand

I am safe and secure in his arms

Not easily shaken

I belong

CHAPTER FOUR:

But God

Freshman year, woohoo! A fresh start. A new beginning. Yall, guess what? I meant to mention that at the end of eighth grade I got all A's. Look at God won't he do it. I thank God for giving me the strength and determination because I serve a God of excellence, so everything that I do has to be unto the Lord with excellence. I love him and want to glorify God in everything that I do. God got my back so I know he will take care of you too. He's simple, just trust him. So freshman year, I worked my butt off to get excellent grades, I had to sacrifice a lot of free time, but It was worth it because it paid off in the end. Also, family time is still important. So make time for that. Always remember that if all you have is Jesus, then that's all you need to live and thrive. I had the best algebra teacher. She made math so fun, her name was Ms.Robertson, She was hilarious. She would relate math to relationships and food. She taught in a way that almost everyone in her class had a high score on the test every time. It was so easy to understand and grasp the concept of algebra one. Best math teacher ever! My grades were good. So I started joining school clubs. I mean it was freshman year. I was new and wanted to make friends, meet new people. One of them was the Cougars for Christ. This meeting was where believers all joined together on Friday mornings and worshiped. They had bible lessons and we ate good food. I loved it. Worshiping God and being around like-minded believers who have a heart for God. It was an amazing experience. I think that was one of the first times that I spoke for a club meeting. It was nice, sharing with others about being the light. I would encourage them to keep worshiping and serving him in everything that we do. I also was a part of the worship team in c4c. It was very humbling. I give God all the glory. The worship leaders Jordan and Ruth were like our worship leader choir mom and dad. They really and truly have a heart for people. My faith really grew my freshman year. I started talking to God more during the summer nights. While watching Todd white on youtube and also going to church. Where I was growing in our walk with the lord. I was afraid at first but I knew that God was with me and would give me the strength to minister to the broken, the lost and the hurt. I wanted to comfort them and let them know that they are loved and not forgotten. That God sees them. To add, we live in a world where people are to themselves. Where they thinks its all about them But as believers we are to be the hands on Jesus. Also, to stay at the feet of Jesus. I remember that I wanted to go on a mission trip so bad that summer, But my mom encouraged me, She said. "High School is like a mission trip, Wherever God has you, He has called you there for a reason. Also, to be the light at your campus and shine Christ light. You have the broken and the lost there, let them know that God loves them and isn't mad at them." I was like wow, I didn't think about it like that. I was delighted to share the gospel. As I loved God, I wanted to do what he called me to do. So I started praying for others in my public high school. I said to God "who do you want me to minister to today? Who do you want me to pray for today? Use me lord. I surrender." God would have me pray for people before class, after class. It was a joy, getting to glorify God in everything that I did. I give all glory to God, not me. I remember one time there was this girl, she was going through a lot at home. When I looked at her, I just knew something was wrong. It was the holy spirit guiding me. She started to open up and share with me what was going on. I prayed for her, her family, etc. Then she said "thank you." I really needed that. I think I said, "All glory to God. It's him using me. " I wanted them to know that God loves them. I prayed for people to be healed. So they can know the love of the father and encounter his love. I remember one time I was in biology class. One time before our lab started I asked the girl if she would like prayer. She said yes and told me who it was for. Then I prayed after she said, (In Tears) "thank you." I appreciate it. I said all glory to God, I just wanted to share the love of God with her. I didn't realize the positive influence that I had on my peers. I would bring my bible to school. Then I started to see my friends bring their Bibles to school. One girl in the c4c club said, " One of the persons who inspired me was Amari. I have seen her pray for the lost and the broken and that's what we're supposed to be doing as believers. We are supposed to tell others the good news and what God has done for them. I admire her and her relationship with the lord. Y'all your girl was in tears, I wasn't expecting that at all. God is so good. He is great. He is my heavenly father, my best friend. You can hear the voice of God too, He speaks to everyone in different ways. Through his words, sermons, people and even movies. He can even use a donkey! If you're willing, he will use you in mighty ways to glorify his kingdom. Nothing is too hard for God. He is with you and He is for you. You are safe and secure in God. God loves you. You are valuable to God. You belong to God, God's got you. Don't worry, don't be afraid. You are strong in the lord. Daily as you surrender to the lord, Allow him to heal your heart. He will use you in mighty ways, to glorify his kingdom. The sky's the limit if you simply test the waters.

"Boys, Boys, Boys"

Did I also mention that as I was doing the lord's work the enemy sent a distraction. The enemy realizes your weakness whether you do or don't. I hadn't fully surrendered that area to God. Y'all know how we can want something so bad, that we'll assume things are from God or try to make things work out the way we want it to.

This can be dangerous because then we try to be in control. We can sometimes think that we don't need God or that God won't do what he promised. BUT THAT IS A LIE FROM THE ENEMY, GOD IS TRUE TO HIS PROMISES. ALL HIS PROMISES ARE YES AND AMEN. FOR GOD GIVES GOOD GIFTS TO HIS CHILDREN. It may not have been when you wanted it to happen because maybe you weren't ready at that time. Maybe you were not mature yet or your heart wasn't in the right posture to receive what God has for you. So I would encourage you to become whole in God, allow God to shape you into the daughter/ son he's called you to be. Allow him to purify you and cleanse you of all that shame. So you can be free. Then when the right friend comes along or as my mom likes to call it "Kingdom connection" then you will be that Godly friend that they were looking for and glorify God together. Keeping Christ at the center, growing in your relationship with the lord. You will compliment each other and they will speak life into you. But at this time, I was young. Still growing in God and wanting a friend so bad that I was willing to settle for God very best for me. So I would spend time with my friend, after school I would talk to him. Again he knew the lord, Ladies please save yourself the trouble. If being friends with a guy causes you to almost lose focus on God then Hunnaie it is not worth your time! Please wait on the Lord because this guy had a really rough background and still needed healing, therapy and was not ready to have a friend at the moment. I would encourage him in the lord but he rarely encouraged me to have a deeper relationship in the lord. I believe that I was just supposed to pray for him and not take things further than that by becoming his friend. Anyone knows that ending a relationship is hard and I knew this wasn't healthy being this relationship. We both were growing in the lord, but not respecting each other's time. We were calling each other almost every hour of the day. I remember my mom even noticed that I was calling him and he was calling me a lot. Then I had started to idolize him, putting him before God because God is a jealous God.

So I had to repent and put God where he rightfully deserved to be. First, the day I told him we couldn't be friends first and how I needed to keep Christ first in my life. I hoped he would respect that. He didn't and when I got home, I started getting all these text messages that you're not a good friend and all kinds of rude messages. He felt rejected just like others had done him in the past. But it was a lot for me, I can't be Jesus, I'm not. I am a Daughter of Jesus Christ, I belong to God. I can't be friends with just anyone. But with the ones who God brings along. But I didn't text him back or anything because then I would be stooping down to his level and that wasn't good. I had to forgive him, so in my quiet time with the Lord, I forgave him and released him unto the Lord. I repented for not wanting to wait on God and seek God on if he was my friend or not. Then spend the rest of that year seeking God and keeping Christ first. Remembering not to let anyone come between me and my relationship with the Lord. Wait on the lord ladies, it will save you a ton of hurt and pain. Also, don't be so hard on yourself, your human not perfect. Just see this as a learning lesson to keep Christ first and seek God in everything. For he desires to spend time with you, to know you and grow with you. As you seek him and get to know him, he will inspire and uplift you in the times when you feel weak. As you draw near to him he will draw near to you and heal your heart. For he is a good father.

"Sophomore and Junior Year"

Time flies by, when you're in high school, Freshman year goes by really fast. Sophomore year, I tried a lot of clubs, so much that I realized I had to drop some clubs. It was too much for me to handle. I barely had time to do homework. I was also taking AP classes. I was super busy and my whap (World History Advanced Placement) class homework took forever to get through. I dropped that class to take a much laid back history class. It was worth it because I Aced it. But this year took an unexpected turn. That I don't think, me or my family was prepared for. That morning was around the first week of school. My mom felt strange. she wasn't acting herself. I knew something was wrong, But we couldn't figure it out. That day we went to school. When we came back home my mom was worried and started panicking, I had never seen her like this. Then our Nanu (aka. Mom's mom) came over and comforted mom assuring her that everything is alright. She was quickly sent to the emergency room. When they came home my Nana told me the doctors said, " My mom was diagnosed with bipolar" I couldn't believe it. I didn't want to believe it. I remember praying day and night for my mom. I started to see myself and my siblings handle it in different ways. My brother was getting in trouble at school, my sister was acting up at home and I was fighting for my mom in prayer. I also was depressed and bullied at this time. But God got us through it all. It was hard seeing my mom like that. It's like she was there but she wasn't. I didn't know what was going on. I asked God "why it was happening." Not blaming God because I knew there had to be a reason, we were going through this. Even though we were going through the hardest seasons of our lives, I could not understand what was going on. I trusted God, I was constantly in the prayer closet. I was pleading for my mom because I knew he was going to get me and my family through this. start to fight for someone you love. He had been too good to us to leave us like this. I remember she even had to go to the hospital again because she was starting to worry. Then my papa had to come and spend time with us. Wow, that was a journey. He didn't have the same standards as us such as watching the same movies or praying together as a family, it was a lot. So we had to find common ground. I remember in the morning when one time we had to stay with Nanu y'all we cried and cried. First off, we were not in our own home and were away from our mom for a while. Then I remember when mom called on the phone. We could barely even talk because we missed her so much. Then a miracle happened. God finally allowed my mom to come home. We were so happy. Things were different, surely my mom started to come back to herself. I thank God for my amazing nanu, papa and friends in her life. They were there for us to pray for our mom and encourage her as she was going through this difficult season. It was a blessing. God was faithful to his promises. Even though you may not understand it, you may not know what's going on, God will see you through. God will give you the strength to overcome, Don't give up. God's got you. Even though you may go through trials and tribulation, God is with you. He will get you through anything you face. Nothing is too hard for God. As you seek him and press in, he will surely see you through. That season helped me stand strong for the next season. It was junior year, let me tell you guys that was one of the hardest seasons. It tested my faith, beliefs and motives. But I thank God for his grace and mercy. I had battled with depression and anxiety a lot this year. It was 2018. It was a lot of days feeling shame, less than. I would be in class and feel like everyone was watching me or staring at me. The enemy almost tried to make me confused, But

I thank God for my mom encouraging me to remember who I am in God. For I had strong roots in God. My not easily shaken faith. Clinging to God in those times made me have so much more respect for God and love him so much more. I read a lot of Philippians and Matthews. Looking at the life of Jesus and what he did. Reading about praising the Lord. Let's look at Paul. He went through a lot, was in chains, yet he still praised God. He was bruised, yet he still honored the Lord with everything within him. So during that time at school, I talked to my counselor a lot. She really helped me get through, encouraged me and letting me know that I will be alright. She helped me see the bright sight of things. To get out of my head and ways, I can work on not overthinking. This was hard, not going to lie(or tell a story as my mom would always say) But I kept my eyes on the lord. My mom will tell me I spend time with God more than anybody, I was constantly in the prayer closet seeking the face of Jesus. Most of the time I would just read a scripture, not really paying attention to what God had wanted me to get out of that scripture for that day. I had tried the soap (Scripture Observation Application and Prayer) method, and it really helped. I was taking each scripture, each text, finding out what God had for me. Asking God for understanding. Though it was a lot, it was worth it because God is worth it. God is my everything. God is my peace, my joy, and strength. He sure gave me the strength to get through that season. If you were to ask me months earlier that I was going to go through that, I would've thought you must be joking. It may be too much for me to handle. But I also learned that God doesn't give us too much to where we can't handle. The enemy loves it when you start to believe that God isn't going to do what he said. For the enemy is the king of discouragement. He tries to make you think that your problems are too big. The enemy is a liar. God is bigger than anything. Greater is he that is in you than he that is in the world. God is greater than fear, worry, depression, depression, and overthinking. God will keep you in perfect peace as your mind stays on him. God is your biggest cheerleader. So I started was reading my word more. Clinging to my heavenly father. Surrendering my all to him, acknowledging that I need him. That I can't do this life without him. He was still faithful to his promises. He did what he said he would do. I thank God for his word because his word is life and a weapon against the enemy. As you fix your eyes on the lord, he can help you overcome the seasons that may be hard. He will help you. Thanking him for the wonderful seasons, where you realized you still needed him. I also thanked God for the harder ones, where I realized you needed him more than ever. He was right there with you always. God loves you so much. He is with you. He is for you. He loves you so much. Let's draw near to the father's heart, dining at the king of kings table. learn who the heavenly father is and who you are in God. He is our security. He is our heavenly father. He is our best friend. He desires to hear from you. He longs for you to spend time with him. To get to know him and be filled with his perfect love, joy and peace. Then you can share this amazing love you have with others. You can let them know that they can have a relationship with the lord and get to know him more. As their heavenly father. Their shepherd. They will not want to even look back. The world leaves you wanting more and more. But Christ satisfies. I'm content in and with God.

"The Move that Changed Everything"

Junior year was almost over. We were about one month from moving. Y'all we had to pray like never before. I submitted my request to the lord and said lord, "your will be done and not my will." God, you are in control. Have your way." Then, one night, we started packing and moving our clothes. Our mom and her friends helped us.Thanks to the help of my brother. He did a great job. We didn't get done till about three o'clock in the morning. There was a lot of stuff to move. We waited in the car and were ready to move. Read to start a new chapter. Ready for a change.

New beginnings were up ahead or so we had expected. Ladies and gentlemen, let me tell you, this I didn't even see coming. It was something out of the ordinary. So this was my senior year. The summer before my senior year of high school and I was moving. Y'all God is not the author of confusion. So what my amazing mom encouraged me to do was spend time with God. Getting direction because as the lord is our shepherd, he is our wise counselor and our heavenly father. He is our peace. So I sought God about what school to go to. Then literally the next day, this lady who used to give us rides to school had stopped. So we started going to Klein High School. So what I did was PRAISE THE LORD, THANK YOU JESUS FOR THE CONFIRMATION! We were so excited to be going to this new school. To start new friendships, meet new teachers. New schedule to memorize, etc. As this was one of the best districts across. I got there. People were friendly and kind. But somehow I was acting shy, feeling less than. I had curled up in a ball, wanting nothing to do with people anymore. People judged me and labelled me but it was because they did not know who they were for. For they were hurting. They didn't know that God loved them. That they have a family and belong in the christ kingdom. That God was enough. That they didn't have to keep striving, but rest in christ. I was like how can people who don't even know me judge me. They assumed something that wasn't even true about me. Nobody has once told me are you okay? or what's going on? But just think they know everything. It was hard at first to handle that. I felt as if I didn't have a voice. I felt overlooked, hidden and lost. I didn't know who I was. For the voices attacked Mr in my mind. To a great extent. I had crippling depression, paranoia and anxiety. I would think, Are they looking at me or judging me. Even a teacher bullied me. I had to move class periods. I was going through alot. I couldn't even pay attention to a dying world around me who needed the lord. Then I wonder how Jesus felt as people said things about him, as people talked about him behind his back. They hardly cared to take the time to get to know him. I had to learn to surrender, but in a whole fresh way. I had to learn God all over again because the enemy had attacked me, but this was out of nowhere. This was coming from a girl who would spend hours in the prayer closet. God is so good. He kept me through all of that. He saved me so many times y'all. I had to remind myself that God loves me daily with scriptures on index cards. I also said it out loud "God loves me" I had to learn who I am all over again. So I could live. To breathe so anxiety wouldn't take me out. I had to know I am chosen by God. I belong to God. The enemy cannot touch me. I had to keep my eyes on the lord. Not worry about people who didn't even create me. I prayed for them. Also, God thinks good thoughts towards me. I am not a mistake. As I thought about the goodness of God. For these challenges made me stronger in the lord. I had allowed God to renew my mind to the image of who he is. Helping me to see the good in everything. Yes this was a process. I started journaling to God. (Highly Recommended) I talked to God. I spent time with him and allowed him to speak to me. aligned my will to his. To live. That God had a purpose for me even in my trials and tribulations. It was the miracle of Jesus Christ that he delivered me a year after high school. I'm living proof that the word works. I give ALL the glory and the Honor to God. Literally, if it wasn't for the grace and mercy of God. All God's want is you. He wants your heart. He wants to spend time with you. He wants you to come to him. So he can fill you. Whether that's five to fifteen minutes of Journaling daily. He will remind you of the promises you made with him years ago. He will amswer. God will draw near to you as you draw near to him. He will embrace you with loving arms. Just come as you are. People think they have to wear their Sunday best when they come to God. The most genuine and humblest man(Jesus Christ) to ever walk this earth. Jesus, he ate with Everyone. He ate with the sinners, the poor, the overlooked, and those who felt forgotten. Jesus wanted them to know that he understands him. He even came to the earth in a barn that probably had animal poop around the floors. Jesus came in such a humble way to this earth. He is so kind, full of mercy and grace. Heyyyyy! Sorry I just wanted to add that, It rhymed. Jesus was human, yet he still was perfect in all he did. He was the messiah. He obeyed his heavenly father and loved him more than anything. We have to get our hunger back for God. We have to surrender our all to him. I encourage you to say "lord I need to help me. Lord, when I am weak you are strong. When I fall you are right there to catch me. Deliver my mind God. Restore my soul to God. Lord, you are welcomed in this place. Fill me with your presence of God. You are my best friend." He will tell you marvelous things you do not know because you love him and desire to get to know him. Also, I have been through the storm and rain. But I thank God for his arms comforting me and my family. God will direct your paths and teach you things that you never knew or saw at the moment.

The chains are broken
by Amari Peters

Dear Lord,

I ask that

You Would

Break every

Chain

Help me to

Peters/Real Seasons of My Life

Remember

That you are

Greater

Stronger

Fear

Can no

Longer

Serve a

Purpose In

My life

Thank you lord

CHAPTER FIVE:

The New Me

These struggles were hard. I didn't know how I would make it. But once I fell in love with the word of God. I would read the love letter my heavenly father wrote to me. His word. It encourages me daily in my walk with the lord. He instructs and guides me. He leads me. God is the word, and his word is alive. It's sharper than a double-edged sword. I put on the armor of God and fought with God. I couldn't do this alone, so I thank God for my amazing counselors. They inspired me to be better. To grow daily and improve in Jesus Christ daily. My first counselor I had. O my gosh!

Y'all She encouraged me to stand firm in the lord and remember who was am in God. She helped me to keep going. To know that I am safe in God. That God wasn't going to hurt me. But hold me and protect me daily. That I am redeemed by the blood of the lamb. I am no longer who I used to be. I am a child of God. I am no longer chained by lust. But a slave to righteousness and holiness. Redeemed and whole. I belong to God. Because the enemy loves to make you feel as if you're alone, as if no one sees you. But my counselor saw the best in me and helped me realize it. That I have the solution to all my problems and that is God. Growing and maturing in my walk with the lord. With the help of Jesus Christ, my mom, friends and mentees, I was on my way to freedom. Thank you Lord for never giving up on me and helping me every step of the way. I want to let you guys know this was not an overnight process. This took time, but it was worth it. Like I once heard the quote saying, "You are worth the investment." Jesus took his time making you. So take time loving and filling yourself with the word of God. Declare the promises of God that you. That you will live and not die and declare the works of the lord. If God be for you who can be against you. The joy of the lord is my strength. This is the day that the lord has made and I will rejoice and be glad in it. you want to be free and live the blessed life that God has called you to live, I encourage you to get in the word and go to therapy. My next counselor Y'all I can't even describe the words of how she addressed the issue and gave me practical tips. Also, that I can apply to keep growing and live the God-ordained life he's called me to live. To flourish. She understood me from a level to where I was like I wanted to change. That I wanted to be better. I was too precious. A diamond in the rough. In counseling things would come up that I didn't know I was dealing with. Counseling helped me get to the root of the issue and how to break those bad habits and thought patterns. To see things from God's perspective and learn to apply the word of God. They brought light to things that I had dealt with. Things that I didn't even know I needed counseling on. From childhood. It was something I had never seen. I thank God so much for showing me he hasn't forgotten me. These were amazing Christian women who loved the Lord with all their heart. I give all the glory, honor and praise to the lord. He is worthy to be praised. I encourage everyone to cherish those moments. Never forget them. You can teach someone else. You can aspire others to be who God has called them to be and that's what I hope this book does.

"Seeds of Faith"

Then when I went back to school the second semester of senior year, something happened. I started reading, applying the word of God and journaling to God. I started to see breakthrough. I wanted to share and open up to others. I wanted to sharing my story with others. For I know how it feelsas if everyone else around you is winning, and getting blessed. Then you're left to the crumbs. I know what it feels like to feel alone as if no one sees you. But let me tell you something, I had learned I had to forgive. So I could be free. I had to forgive those who hurt me, who shamed and condemned me. My mom would always tell me, "He can't have your joy, If he didn't give it to you, He can't take it away." I never forgot that. That is so true. Why would I get mad at imperfect people who had flaws and were human? I had to give them to Jesus, saying. "Lord I am not in control, bless them and keep them lord. In Jesus name amen." Once I did that. The Lord lifted the burden off me. Once you forgive somene you may have to say it multiple times. Don't worry about it. you must believe and trust God that he said he will do what he promised. Pray that God will heal their heart and restore them. That they know that God loves them. In Matthew 11:23-30 "Come to me, all you who are weary and burdened, and I will give you rest. Take my yoke upon you and learn from me, for I am gentle and humble in heart, and you will find rest for your souls. For my yoke is easy and my burden is light." As we come to God, humble open and transparent Then God will do his part. He will began to mature you. That comes with a willing surrender heart. You have to be willing to obey God and honor God. To praise him for who he is. To seek him intentionally because you love him. This may take time, but the more you surrender, God will begin to fill you. All his promises are yes and amen. God is not a god that he shall lie. He is the truth, and the truth will set you free. Who the Son sets free is free. How can you be free if you don't know the truth? We must daily get our word. It is life and a weapon. It is our sword. It is our guide, our peace, and protection. We must daily allow the word of God to renew our minds and restore our souls. Teaching us how to become one with him. God has never given me a spirit of fear but of power, love and a sound mind. Remember that Jesus is your prince of peace. Come to him. He longs to hear from you. If You're struggling with hearing from God, talk to God. Tell him what's on your heart. Philippians 4:6-7 says. "Don't be anxious about anything but in every situation by prayer and petition with thanksgiving present your requests to God. And the peace of God, which transcends all understanding, will guard your heart and mind in Christ Jesus." Tell God everything. He is our heavenly father and best friend. Tell him what's on your heart. Be real. He knows what you're thinking already. But he wants to hear from you. Believe the truth about who God says you are and most importantly who God is. Pray constantly. Tell God what you need. He is our shepherd and want to take care of his children. He cares for you. When you hurt, he's hurt. Thank God for all he's done, remember the goodness of God. Thank God for his grace and mercy. He didn't have to save me, but he did. Come on, somebody. I thank God for helping me to change my ways. He helped me to see things from his perspective. He is learning the heart of God. What he likes and what he does not like. Having that deep relationship with the lord. Once you surrender then will fill you with His peace and joy. God's got you and he will keep you in perfect peace as your mind stays on him because he loves you.

Blessed and know the best is yet to come. That you will come up out of this. You will make it. You will live.

"Influencing"

The beginning of my senior year may have been rough. But God has the final say. What the enemy meant for evil, God turned it around and worked out everything for my good. I started getting into bible-based clubs, sharing my testimony. It blessed many people. They applied the tools and found it to be very successful. They prospered as they allowed the word of God to fill them. God is in control. God is greater than anything. God can take something and make it beautiful. He took all the bad out and put something beautiful in you. Your heart of Gold. Papas heart. I just wanted to encourage you. You're an overcomer. You are prosperous in everything that you do. Jesus will help you, Philippians 4:19 says, "you can do all things through Christ who gives you strength." You can overcome anything with God. Just like I overcame depression and anxiety, so can you. With God, you will heal. You will make it. You are victorious . You are a winner. You will win. Please, I encourage you to take the words of affirmationsand say them yourself speak life. Watch God move by your faith. He did it for David, Daniel and Joseph. He will surely do it for you. Sometimes we forget these were ordinary people. Anyone can apply these steps and be free. As I used my gift, im sure the lord will use me in miraculous ways. This was a lot of pressure, following the lord in this world. But remember that God is with you and you are here for his purpose. I think all your imperfections are beautiful. It's what make you beautiful. God will always encourage you. Let your hope be built on Jesus- My pastor once said. We need to get back to our first love. our firm foundation. Jesus Christ, our savior. Our healer. Our deliverer. As you allow him into your life, he will restore those places that were once broken and make them whole. Helping you to grow, teaching you how to seek him intentionally. But you have to want it. You have to want to be healed and set free. Want revival to take place in your heart, So you can see it take place in others. It starts with you. God can use just one person to glorify his kingdom. To be the chain breaker. To minister to nations. To travel the world telling others about the delightful news. We need to get in our word daily. We need to know God for ourselves. It is crucial to keep God first in this hour. To get back to the father's heart. To be daily filled with his perfect love. Let God's peace which surpasses all understanding come into your heart. Knowing that God is greater than anything. God is with you. God will never leave you. God is a restorer. He can take those things that were once broken and lost. He can make them whole. God hasn't forgotten you. He sees you at this moment. He has you in the palm of his hand. You shall live and not die and declare the works of the lord. You will make it. As you keep your eyes on the Lord trusting that he's got you, then God will bless you beyond measure to be a blessing unto others. The best is yet to come. You are enough in God. You are qualified through christ. God is an expert at purifying, cleansing, and healing. So you can be the person who God has called you to be. Trust in God the word works. Don't let others get you down or stop you from doing what God has called you to be. Trust God.

"Tell Someone"

I know I talked about knowing who you are and things such as that. But God wants you to be free. Free from people taking advantage of you. That victim mentality. So I encourage you to go talk to someone whether that is your mom or pastor. Don't live alone. Reach out to me. Let them know what you're going through. Nine times out of ten they have been through what you've been through. They can help you. They will encourage you to know that you are too precious to be thinking less of yourself. You are too valuable to think of yourself as worthless. You are too self aware of yourself in Christ to be a people pleaser. You are worth more than gold. You belong to God. God's got you. You are an overcomer. You are God's masterpiece. You are blessed. You will make it through this it is only a season, Don't be afraid to speak out. The enemy makes you feel you're all alone, but that is a lie. There are many people that have been through what you've been through. I've experienced a lot. From homelessness, friends leaving and getting bullied. But I wanted you to know that if God is for you not against you. No weapon formed against you shall prosper, you shall live and not die. You will make it. The word of God is a lamp unto your feet and a light unto your path. As you cling to God seeking him, daily surrendering to him allows him to speak through you through his word, a song etc. Watch God have his way and move in your life. He want the best for you. I'm not just saying that, But I mean it. I want you to succeed. I know that if God can do it for me, he can do it for you.

God is enough
by Amari Peters

He is all I need

He is my

everlasting peace

He is my

comfort in need

There is

No one

like him

He never leaves

Peters/Real Seasons of My Life
Never shames

Never lies

He is all truth

He is my savior

Rescued me from death

From the enemies snaring traps

That I couldn't see

He is for me always

He is my comfort

_____

CHAPTER SIX:

Remember Who You Are

It is vital for you to know who you are. To remember who and whose you are. To honor God in all that you do because you love him. You obey him. Some of us want to but it's hard. It's hard if you only say it's hard. Keep our eyes on Jesus Christ. Our lord and savior. Our best friend. If you draw near to God he will draw near to you. As you cling to the father, run to him with open arms. He will keep you safe. Nothing could ever pluck you from his hand. God's got you. You will make it. Weeping may endure for a night, but joy comes in the morning. The joy of the Lord is your strength. Christians should be one of the happiest people on this earth because we have the living God on the inside of us. Who is full of Joy. As we dine at the father's feet wanting nothing more but to sit at his feet, he will fill us with his fullness. Sometimes just sit in his presence and bask in his glory. We remember that even though earth may pass away, but the word of God will be everlasting. God is life. We need to allow God to renew our mind, so we can get a clear vision of what he wants us to do. Get disciplined child of God. The time is now. We need to get knowledge because God says my people are destroyed for lack of knowledge. Imagine how much freedom we could experience if we were to get knowledge, know the truth, and maintain our freedom through Christ. Through these steps, in the next chapter, I will give practical and simple tips on how you can live the blessed life that God has called you to live. It may not happen suddenly, but with time and patience God will bring it to fruition. You must trust God. Through the good and bad. Pray and seek his face turn from your old ways. But first, let's explain the importance of giving.

"Serving, Glorifying God"

As I learned who I am, I also served more. I gave back even more to my community. There's always someone who may be in a tougher situation than you. We can always pray for them or help them out. We are the salt of the earth. But if the salt loses its flavor how can it be made salty again? It is no longer good for anything, except to be thrown out and thrown out. You are the light of the world. We are to glorify God in everything that we do. When people see us they should see Jesus. They should see the heart of the father in us. We live in a world where people want things now and want more. But God Is like what about me? Have you become so full of foolish worldly ways, conforming to the patterns of this world that you've forgotten the one who created you? Don't you know that I am your provider? That I am your peace, your shepherd. That you don't have to worry about your next month's payments because I've already got that taken care of. That I will never leave you nor forsake you, That I will give you exactly what to say. You won't have to worry or fear because God is your perfect peace and your guide. He will never lead you astray. Let God be in control. You can't do this on your own. It's time to let go and Let God. He knows what's best. Yes as he cares for the lilies and the birds and trees. He will surely take care of you. Now serving won't just be a checklist, but a heart posture. You get to serve Jesus every day because you have a relationship with him. You don't have to worry about hiding under shelter like some counties have to. I remember one time I spoke in front of my FCA club, this was after junior year, and all that had happened. Y'all I was nervous. But I learned that as I come to him, he will keep me in perfect peace as my mind stays on him, So I won't have to worry or doubt because he will lead me. He will give Mr exactly what he wants to say. Y'all when I tell yall I used scripture that's basically all I used and took notes on my handwritten bookmarks for my bible. Then the holy spirit was moving and touched their hearts. One of our sponsors said she used the applications I had mentioned, and she said she saw a change. I give all glory to God. My heavenly father. My best friend. I encourage you to say "lord use me, say you want to say move if you want to move lord. Help me become in sync with the holy spirit. To become one with the holy spirit. To have that zeal, a strong foundation in the lord. Help me to not even want to go back but keep moving forward. I need you, Lord; I repent of all my sins. I give Fill in the blank to you, lord. I can't do this on my own. Lord you are the great I am. Do what only you can do lord. I surrender my all to you, Lord. Fill me with your truth. Your perfect love that casts out all fear. Thank you lord for peace. Have your way o God. Do what only you can, lord. Help me Lord to stand on your promises. Help me, Lord, to fight the good fight and finish strong. Help me, lord. I need you. Helping others know about the goodness of Jesus. In Jesus Mighty name Amen." Let's be real if it's a struggle to spend time with God. You have to find time, read the word. Jesus took the time for you. He died for you so you can be free. The least we can do is give him a few minutes. He wants us to bless. You deserve to be happy. You deserve good things. As we give our all to him, he will show us what a joy it is being his Daughter/Son. He loves you so much.

"Teach Others"

I just wanted to let y'all know that I'm not perfect. I am human and make mistakes. But there is a God who sent his only son Jesus Christ. Who was bruised, hurt and wounded for you. So you and I could be free healed. He helped me to get back up, fight the good fight. He is continually renewing uds. His word is your strongest weapon. Mine was finising thjs book. The enemy tried to lie to me. He tried fo tell me that no one is going to read your book. No ones going to buy it. But look at God. My uncle bought the kindle version. He also said that I wouldn't be able to finish this book. That I have special needs. Now look at me I'm teaching, speaking and praying peoplr all over the world. You cannot let no one stop you from achieving your goals and dreams. As you get in his word,

He will teach you his ways. He will restore those places in you. So here are a few scriptures you can meditate on getting guidance and direction from the father. Scripture: "You are God's masterpiece." Ephesians 2:10 Observation: We are created in Christ Image. Created by God. God loves us so much he calls us his masterpiece. We are God's prized possession. We are priceless. Created by love. To love. We are perfect in God's eyes. The Lord only satisfies us completely. Application: I am to Let God be the author in my life and write my story. I am to let him paint this picture of surrender, a journey of falling at the feet of Jesus. Trusting God. Letting him be in control of my heavenly father. I am to keep my eyes stayed upon the lord. The author and finisher of my faith. I am to remember daily who I am in God. Standing firm in the lord. Confident in who God created me to be. A Daughter/Son of God. I am to allow God to be God in my life. Let him speak to me either through his word or through people. Remembering that I am set apart for Christ kingdom. That I belong to God. I am chosen by God. I am a child of God. I am set apart for christ kingdom. I am a king's kid. I am the apple of God's eye. I am to daily meditate on the word of God. It is a Manual about life. My identity is rooted in God. Not a man, nor material things that are temporary or even the angels they are messengers from the lord. We are to worship God only. We are to put our trust in God alone.

For he is limitless. You got to stop putting limits on yourself. God has called you to be great. To reach the nations. Its time for you to come forth. You are worth more than a nine to five. You got billion dollar ideas in you. Rise up woman/man of God. Your time is now.

Prayer: Dear God, help me trust you. Help me to love you God more than anything. Standing on your promises. Trust that you are God alone. Help me Lord to not to the left or right, but keep my eyes stayed upon you lord. My heavenly Father, God, I need you. Lord, I depend upon you lord. Lord, I put my trust in you lord. Guide me and lead me lord. You are my shield. You are my peace. Help me Lord to know that my identity is found in you, Jesus.

Help me Lord to be filled with your truth. Lord, it says in your word that I am a child of God. Help me, Lord, to get into alignment with the word of God. Help me God to do what you've called me to do. I depend on you. Lord, you are my strength. Lord, I thank you for guiding me and leading me on your right path. Lord help me in my business. Help me write more books for your glory. Help me reach more people in Jesus name Amen. Gratitude: Thank you for this day. Thank you Lord that you are my shepherd. Thank you Lord I am your beloved and you are mine. Thank you Lord for creating me and giving me life. Thank you Lord for renewing my mind about who you say I am. I am strong. I am resilient. I have the mind of christ. I will be excellent in all I do with Christ's help. Thank you for uprooting the enemies lies. I am not ugly. I am beautiful or handsome. I am not a mess. I am a blessing and what I have to say is important. I am not forgotten. God sees me and he loves me dearly. I am the apple of God's eye. I am blessed and highly favored. I will live a long life. I will live to see my grandchildren's children. Thank you for helping me to remember that I am defined by you lord. Help me God to not look to the left or right but to keep my eyes stayed upon you lord. Thank you Lord for seeing the best in me. For wanting me. Accepting me. Thank you Lord for everything because it drew me to your love. To You. Here's another scripture to encourage you: "Therefore, if anyone is in Christ, the new creation has come:(a) The old has gone, the new is here." 2 Corinthians 5:17 Observation: As you repent of your sins, pray and seek the face of the father, turning from your wicked ways. Inviting God into your heart. He comes into your heart and helps you to live life in freedom unto him. Free from the chains of guilt, shame, anger, hurt, rage and condemnation. He heals and restores your heart to wholeness daily. Little by little day by day. Application: I am to yield myself to the daily. God got me and he won't let me down. I am to allow God to heal my heart. Let him into the deep parts of my heart and be vulnerable to him. Helping me to grow and mature into the person he's called me to be. I am to surrender my old self, ways, and habits to the lord. I am to remember that I am a new creation in Christ. I'm set apart. Not saying that I'm better than anyone, but I know who I am in God. I am a new changed person for the better. God has new relationships, new beginnings in store for me, and healthy relationships. I will be an excellent steward over being a sympathetic friend. Loving that person with Christ and praying for that friend daily. Reminding them of the promises of God in their life. Seeing the best in them. And as you allow Christ to fill you with his presence. Fearing God. Being in awe of him. His love. His presence. Who he is. You will mature and blossom into the daughter/ Son of the king he's called you to be. Again you're not striving but thriving. In progression not perfectionism. Pray: Lord My heavenly father, I come before you and I ask for your forgiveness. I turn from my old ways that were not pleasing in your sight. I need you, lord. I can't make it without you lord. I ask that you come into my life. Purify my heart of God, from all iniquity, and fill me with your presence. I surrender lord my all to you lord and I ask that you will cleanse me and wash me in your word. Help me to get to know who you are. Help me to not even want to desire to do what I used to do, watch or act. Help me to truly live for you lord. I need you lord. I'm tired of doing things my way, I'm ready to live for you Jesus. Have your way in me Jesus Christ the messiah. Lord, you are in control of my life. Show me how to do life with you, to thrive and flourish in who you called me to be. Help me lord. Help me Lord to trust you, to allow you to be God. I am tired of running. I lay at your feet, resting in your presence, knowing that you've got me. Guide me and lead me lord. In Jesus name Amen. As you guys daily take the word of God and meditate on it piece by piece, section by section. Word by word. Looking up definitions, the context, really diving into the word of God. Getting that guidance, revelation, peace, and breakthrough that you've been searching for is in the word. As you daily, morning and night Fill your mind, will, and emotions with the word of God. Aligning to his perfect will in your life. Letting him be God alone. Your provider. Your Peace. Your Strength. Your Joy. Your Guide. Developing that firm foundation with God and keeping God first in everything. You will learn how to live a blessed life through christ. As you fully surrender, every area of your life to God and communing with him twenty- four seven. Keep applying and continue applying the word of God. Maturing in your walk with the lord. God is for you and not against you. Rest. Be still. And learn in his presence.

"The Power of Speaking Life"

If you stand for nothing , you'll fall for everything. But when you believe the word of God, stand on it. Applying his powerful promises. You will see breakthroughs. As you put Christ first, daily saying "God what's on your heart today?" what do you want me to do. Lord, you are in control. Have your way, Lord. Show me how to genuinely love others with Christ's love. How to genuinely give, serve, and sacrifice. Thinking of others, being considerate, while taking care of ourselves. Help us lord stand on the word of God. Help me Lord to keep my eyes stayed upon you lord. My heavenly father. Lord, you have direct access to the throne of my heart. Help me Lord to stand on your promises remembering who you are. Help me to remember that I find my identity in you. That the evil one(The enemy) cannot have me. I belong to God. My heavenly father. As you begin to stand on the promises of God. Applying these principles you will rise. you will prosper in your mind, body, and soul by taking care of the temple that God has given you. Knowing his voice is his word. If you want to hear his voice, spend time in his presence, his word. Put on some worship music. Developing that relationship with him. One thing most people don't get to experience, the fullness of God, is because the first thing they do is make excuses. I can't do this or this is hard. If you want freedom you will do sme desperate, yet rewarding things for God. For example, studying and praying for hours. Praying until chains of what once held you down, breaks off of you. Then God's like I took the time to die for you, So why do you sacrifice a little of your time to spend with me. God says in his word, if you love me you'll obey me. When you surrender your life to Jesus. You're saying that you're committed to the lord, your shepherd. Your protector, defender. Trusting that he will do what he said. As you love the lord, you'll want to make time for him, to dine in his presence. To dine at his feet. You will began to hear God more clearer. Ypu will be filled with his perfect love and encounter his fullness. Letting God speak life and wisdom in his word. It may not be easy. But as long as he sees that you're willing, making time, putting in the effort to spend time with him. Then he will draw near to you, sharing his heart with you. Telling you things you may not know. At first the word may be hard to understand but as you allow God to renew your mind, from that clouded mindset and ask him for wisdom, for understanding, for revelation. In the bible, James 1:5 "if any of you lacks wisdom, you should ask God, who gives generously to all without finding fault and it will be given to you." So I encourage you to ask your heavenly father, Who longs to hear your voice. To Get to know his child. His beloved. His son. God sees you. God notices you. You are the head and not the tail, above and not beneath. God loves you. You are fearfully and wonderfully made in Christ's image. You have a sound mind in Jesus Christ the messiah. You are enough. You don't have to prove yourself to people. You are not worthless. But worthy to come and sit at the feet of Jesus. You are a blessing to others. You are blessed. In the next section I will give you a list of affirmations to use daily. You can declare them boldly in the morning or at night. Speaking life the promises of God over your life. Reminding yourself of who God has called you to be. A Daughter or Son of the most high king. You will see a change in about 21 days. The more you are consistent. The more you will start to see change and grow in the way you carry yourself, the way you see yourself. As Christ loved. Royalty. Not to be treated any kind of way because you are precious in God's eyes. A queen/King. God's beloved. As you meditate on his promises and apply the word of God, you will start to mature into the Godly woman/Godly man that God called you to be. Being the best version of the new and improved you. You are worth the investment. As you become the best of who you are in God, then you will begin to see the best in others. Not only will you start to see a change in your life but you will begin to see a change in the lives of those around you. For your mind, relationships, finances and family will get better and prosper in Jesus name.

Peters/Real Seasons of My Life
"Affirmations"

Here is a list of daily affirmations that will remind you of who God says you are, reminding you you are not defined by what others have spoken over you, you are not defined by what your parents have spoken over you. You are defined by who God says you are. You are a child of God.

You are the apple of God's eye, hidden in the shadow of his wings (Prov 17:8)
You are united with Christ and one with him in spirit (1 Corinth. 6:17)
You are born of God and the evil one cannot touch you (1 John 5:18)
You will find grace and mercy in time of need (Hebrews 4:16)
You are God's temple (1 Cor 3:16)
You may approach God with freedom and Confidence (Ephesians 3:12)
You are God's work of art, created to do good works (Ephesians 2:10)
You are adopted as God's child (Ephesians 1:5)

The good work that God has begun in you will be completed (Phil 1:6)
You've been forgiven of all of your sins. The debt of sin against you has been canceled (Colossians 1:13-14)
You've been given a spirit of power, love and self-discipline (2 Timothy 1:7)
You are holy and blameless (Ephesians 1:4)
You are fearfully and wonderfully made in Christ image (Psalm 139:14)

Unto The Lord
by Amari Peters

Lead me to others

Who were broken

In need of

Compassion

That they never

Received

Lives were

Touched

Let Them Know

It wasn't me

But it was

My prince of Peace

My Everlasting Joy

It was Christ

Flowing

Through me

CHAPTER SEVEN:

All Glory to God

Can I be real with you guys? There were days where I wanted to quit, where I wanted to give up and throw in the towel. Then God was like who's going to fill in the gap that only I've given you to be the solution to someone's problem. Who's going to speak the truth? Who's going to do what I've specifically designed them to do. The word of God is life and a weapon. Who's going to teach others how crucial it is to read and declare the word of God. Y'all it is worth it. If I can reach just one person. Helping them in their journey with the lord. Getting free from anxiety, depression and suicidal thoughts. Then that is okay with me because all it takes is just one person to teach another and reach millions. I do this not for my benefit but for the glory of God. He gets all the glory, all the honor and all the credit. I couldn't have done it without him.

He is my savior, my healer, my deliverer. Just as he is this for me, He is this for you too. God is the same God as he was yesterday. I remember one time I was going through a tough time and my Christian club sponsor told me, "When you can't seem to figure it out, just surrender, saying lord I need you have your way in me lord and what are you trying to teach me through all this" Do you know when I applied them using the word of God, My life changed I started to see a shift in the way I walked in the hallways, the way I talked, my perspective changed, I started to see the good in everything, The way I thought about myself, the way I went about things, being mindful of what I thought. I daily needed to repent and turn to God allowing him to get to the root of the issue in me through counselors, my mom. Friends etc. and heal me from any past trauma. That my mom is doing the best she can to raise us. She loves me and she cares. I needed to hear that. My brother is doing well. My sister is doing well. My mom is healthy. I cannot complain. I thank God daily. Because I wouldn't have been here today, if it wasn't for his grace and mercy. Also I praise God for my mother's prayers and sacrifices. Thank you lord.

"Next Steps"

As I love to encourage others and see the best in others. I have also had the opportunity to minister and encourage others, letting them know that they are not alone. So I recommend, if you'd like to, follow my youtube channel @Amariiman you will find videos about how not worry and how to be financially wise in 2025. Wow that rymes. is about inspiring young millennials in knowing who they are. That their worth is found in Jesus Christ. Who loves them, wants the best for them, and sees the best in them. He doesn't shame or condemn, But is full of grace and mercy. I was also taught how to declare the word of God, How to use the word of God. To Know who they are and Whose they are, As children of the most high God. I encourage you to check it out. You will not want to miss it. Also as I love to write because I didn't used to like to write. Once I realized I have to write thousands and thousands of college in papers, I was like I need to love to write and once I started writing daily, being intentional about it and doing it for the glory of God. I started to love writing, as I began to pick up the pen and just let the Lord have His way in me, it was amazing. Thank the lord because A girl didn't know what to say, but Jesus Christ knew exactly what to say.

So I even went ahead and started a blog, where I write pure real authentic poems I telling real stories in my life of his everlasting love. Its on wordpress. Its called Real seasons of my life. It is inspired by God. He is my heavenly father. My prince of Peace. Just as I can do all things through Christ who gives me strength, My sister, my brother from another mother. So can you. Start that book, start that business, start that blog, that podcast, or art studio you've always wanted to build. You can do it. Like Nike said, "Just Do It"

"Congrats"

O my gosh! Guys did you enjoy this book or what? I am finally done with the chapters. I give all glory to God, never in a million years would I have ever thought I would be writing a book. I pray you enjoy this book and find it very helpful. Apply these life-changing tips that will have you living your blessed life. As surely It did mine. Continue to get in the word daily. It is Powerful. As much as we think about food, we should be thinking about the word our daily bread. Facts! Anyways, As you meditate daily on the word of God, Focusing your attention on him, instead of giving in to fear, worry, or doubt. Or Insecurity. God is the prince of peace. He will never leave you nor forsake you. He's got you. He has great plans in store for you. You are going to be okay. I'd never thought that God would use me as a shy, little and insecure person from Texas, who thought nobody even cared about her, Felt worthless, like nobody cared, always feeling overlooked. Started blossoming into a mature God-fearing young woman. Blessing thousands of people worldwide. I give all glory to God, knowing that I am a child of God, So Can You! If he can do it for me, he can surely do it for you. How bad are you willing to fight for your freedom? For your peace. A Sound Mind. Joy. Strength. Clarity. Direction. I encourage you to share this book with anyone who may go through hard times, depression, or anxiety, letting them know that they are not alone and there is someone who cares about them. I would've loved to have this book when I was young, It would have saved me from so much hurt and pain. So share this, let's encourage each other, grow stay tuned for more books, for sure devotionals. Also share and tag your story on my instagram @Amariimanco using the hashtag #RealseasonsbyAmari. Remember the sky is limitless, if you test the waters. Blessings. Know that I don't consider myself a celebrity just as a servant of Christ. A child of God. I want to do what God has called me to do to Glorify his kingdom. To honor him above all else. Y'all he's been so good to me. He has been such a gentleman. He has always seen the best in me, even when others didn't. When they thought I would never be great or do anything great. Always looking down on my plans. But they didn't have the same vision dream I had, so they couldn't go where I was going. I had better things to do. I was going places. I rarely had friends. But I always have Jesus Christ, My Lord and savior. My best friend. Who never stops loving me. Never stopped giving up on me.

Acknowledgments

I want to acknowledge first God that he has helped me more than I can count. I want to thank my mom for being my mother and her wise nuggets. I want to thank Anyah my twin for always believing in me and Elijah for your funny jokes and Xavier for always being a listening ear when I needed you. Love you, bro.

Author Bio

Amari Peters has always loved to write when she was young. When she and her family would have their family devotionals, they would write and talk to God. She always had plenty of journals growing up that express herself well through her writing. Her mom would always say writing helps you get thoughts on words you didn't know how to articulate onto paper. Amari loves to write because she loves to inspire and encourage young Millenials in her walk with the lord and share her struggles and triumphs to help others to know that they are not alone, to see them succeed, and inspire them to do what they love to do.

Amari Peters is a senior in High School and lives in beautiful Texas with her amazing family. She writes nonfiction books and Devotions about Faith. Helping others to grow and deepen their relationship with the Lord.

Made in the USA
Coppell, TX
12 April 2025

48222195R00066